nuclear oran

Cupid is Tl

by
Christopher
Michael

Release Date January 7th, 2017

Published by:

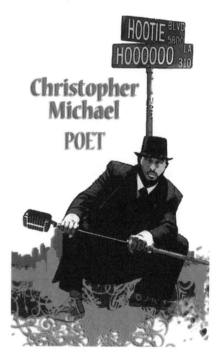

Printed in the United States of America
2nd Edition
SML 04212007
CLK 04302007
ISBN 0-9984270-0-4
Published by 310 Brown Street
www.310brownstreet.com
www.mrmichael310.com

Christopher Michael

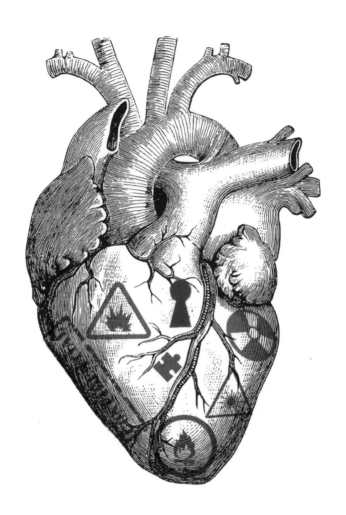

Nuclear Orange

DEDICATION

This book is dedicated to me, because I earned it. I did not do it alone, not all the inspiration was self-generated but this one,
is for me.

SOME OF THESE POEMS

Some of these poems might come from a real place based on actual events.

Some of these poems may be dramatized with a touch of exaggeration.

Some of these poems may be completely fabricated.

Some of these poems may be pure unadulterated truth.

GRATITUDE

To my homes away from home: Under One Roof, Killeen Poetry Slam and Austin Poetry Slam, Austin NeoSoul and The Poetic Sweet Spot.

Thank you Lord for this talent and I pray someone is touched by the words you bless me with.

Haiku

The haiku featured
in this book are non-traditional.
(so calm down)

Christopher Michael

I've heard,
that words don't matter.

Then why,
did God use them to make all of creation?

We poets,
merely children playing with daddy's tools.

The pen,
the deadliest of spears we cut life into paper.

The stage,
the shoes he leaves at the door we're just trying to stand in.

The mic,
his hammer heavy to lift but we keep trying.

We poets!
We gods!
We children of the Most High!

How dare you mortals tell God how to speak?

~Christopher-Michael

Contains, But Not Limited To:

Christopher Michael

-*I*-
Tea eM Eye

hai·ku
俳句

Poetry,
not marketed mainstream.
It won't fit inside a (w)rapper.

My mom
smacked me into the middle of next week.
Time travel
is real.

FA·THER

noun   fa·ther   \ˈfä-thər

DEFINITION

1:   A man who has begotten a child.

2:   A man who shows up and takes responsibility.

3:   An unwitting centurion compelled to watch off-spring sleep with the goal of ensuring they take that next breath. Staring at their rising chest as if reading God's warranty that father will never see his tomorrow's last breath.

4:   A man that bounds out of bed as if to catch the thief in the night risking midnight sacrifices of pinky toes, on the altar of dresser legs and door jams in ebony painted, shadow scarred rooms, just to see a glimpse of his future.

When a man would rather watch the peace on the face of his child as it sleeps, than watch weekly wars, with other men, waging battle over balls.

That man,

> *is in love.*

10

Christopher Michael

IMAGINE

I was born a bastard shortly after my daddy was drafted. It must have been a rough draft, spilling the blood of fellow man in foreign land fighting side by side with brothers who will never again hold family in hand. They must have been some of the greatest soldiers that ever lived. 'Cause the politicians we elected erected a great stone tablet made of granite and forever etched their names in it. Fifty-eight thousand one hundred and seventy-seven of them spilled their blood in foreign lands thousands of miles from home and I grew up, never knowing if my father was a poet or just some poem. 'Cause nobody ever helped me get to know him.

I was left to imagine him in the only way that I know how. So imagine being a poet forced to write a poem you don't even believe in, drafted to spit lines, to spill ink for inconceivable reasons. Then come home from foreign stages only to have the poetry you thought you were defending spit on your pages. The worst part is that most of these poets wat'n spittin' lines to take lives, they were spittin' lines to save lives, save the lives of fellow poets as they write side by side.

Imagine an 18 year old poet who can't even finish writing his poem because his ink is running dry looking in your eye screaming for his mommy as you beg God, "Why?" 'Cause you realize he won't survive the end of this rhyme. Then imagine living minute to minute terrified that the next line might be written for you and trusting the aim of your poet's pen is the only thing that will get you through. Then imagine carrying the ink soaked pages of a poem that just took a verse in the head for you and all you can do is keep fighting, all you can do is keep writing. Spitting lines to hold the line, spitting lines to save lives, all the while praying God won't let your ink run dry. Praying you can finish writing your own poem before your ink runs dry and I...

11

I'm that poem at home he didn't even know he wrote. I grew up never knowing if my father was a poet or just some poem, 'cause nobody ever helped me get to know him.

So, I imagined he must have been among some of those poets who managed to escape the reality of the brutality of poets killing poets. I can see him passing around the open mic and smoke it like every breath made life all right. And I suppose some had a deeper pain that gave them the need to mainline metaphors straight to vein. Three decades later how many still carry the pain? The greatest of our poets are immortalized in stone but what of those who survived and don't even have a home.

I once saw a soldier; I mean a poet on the corner opposite some kid selling rocks. I know he was a poet 'cause he had a haiku written on the side of a cardboard box. It read:

> "Help Vietnam Veteran
> Homeless Will Work For Food
> Thanks And God Bless."

He was filthy disheveled a mess but a man, correction; a poet none the less and all he has, to show for his mental, physical and emotional scars is a bowl of lucky charms, filled with Purple Hearts and Bronze Stars and most of you, I mean most of us pass by him and don't even bother but that poet, correction; that soldier could have been your father!

. . .

Christopher Michael

THE BOYS

Cute and cuddly at birth
they roam the Earth
consuming everything in their path.
They are a drain on your financial resources
and in your home, will destroy everything you have.

They can suck the life out of you
like leeches and Langoliers[1]
literally eating your time.

They are the personification of selfishness
and narcissism
making demands
with whining and wailing
like they learned their tympanic torture technique,
from the mythical Banshee Beast
and Siren song that sent sailors crashing to their doom.
As if God refuses to let you sail through life
without any emotional wounds.

Just when you think you've heard,
the snap
of your very last nerve
and you're ready to give one of those little monsters exactly
what they deserve,

                    they smile.

As if the only way you can learn appreciation is through pain,
like the cracking open of your chest,
a necessary stress
so one of them
can place a small fuzzy little tickle in your heart.

14

Christopher Michael

There is nothing like being a father when you see your child smile.
It's like the Earth slows its rotation
so the sun can shine on you for a few minutes more,
like joy sprang to life and knocked on your door.
Forget oil, politics and religion,
preserving those smiles is the only reason a man should go to war.

God,
has smiled on me,
like sun
casting the shadows that are my sons
and I pray for the day I'm out shined by shadows,
my sons,
my seeds,
my future.

I can't live forever so they are the reality to my immortality,
my footprints in the sand of history allowing me to see beyond
the horizon of time. They extend my reach by generations,
they are the solution to my limitation,
my fruit on the family tree.
As long as their chromosomes ask "Y"
there you'll find me.
23 pieces of my puzzle I had the pleasure to pass on and I just pray
they got the best parts of me.

Happiness,
is loving your children.

Joy,
is when they love you back.

Freedom,
can be found in the tear that falls free from a father's face.

15

A man crying for his boys is an Amazing kind of Grace.
If hope floats,
it can be found floating in the brown pools of my eyes.
I keep my eye on them
because they,
are the prize!

1. Langoliers refers to a mini-series by Stephen King in 1985 where we see creatures that eat all that time has left behind.

Christopher Michael

NOT A THIEF

When I was just a wee lad I started to steal GoBots and Transformers from grocery stores. It was a simple case of supply and demand.

I had a high demand for toys
and a low supply of cash.
I took what didn't belong to me,
I was thief,
I was wrong.

When you take someone's something that doesn't belong to you, you are wrong. But you know that. When you stalk a human to incapacitation and penetrate them like an ATM with unlimited withdrawals you are wrong.

You know that!

But YOU, are not a thief.

You are the babysitter that introduced me to porn mags and had me touch her in the closet at 10. You are the downstairs neighbor who introduced a 13-year-old to porn movies and naked breasts live and in the flesh.

Did you fail to get permission?
If you light the flames of passion with someone too drunk,
too young
or too afraid to say yes,
you are not a thief.

You are Columbus with smiles and blankets. You are no Jedi the way you mind trick with comfort and compliments you are a coward.

You are the dark side of Dr. Huxtable, a phantom menace no

Nuclear Orange

one sees or wants to see until 50 years past the statute of limitations.

She is not an open candy jar at the doctor's office. She will notice every piece you take. Your sweet tooth is a fang filled with consequences. How many souls are wedged between your teeth? How many lives have decayed in your molars?

You dentist, hunting for sport blaming Cecil or Leo the lion for wandering into your killing field, you silenced his roar.

He is not a car to be hot-wired
entered
and rode without permission.

You are not a thief, cutting off your hands would be more mercy than you deserve.

You are a politician's promise. You are Bush stealing an election, with the power to steal power making you more powerful.

One cannot create power. One can only take power and add it to self.

You oil company taking and taking leaving behind poison and emptiness.

You super power taking culture and replacing it with democracy WITHOUT PERMISSION!

This is a simple case of supply and demand. You have a high demand for power and a low supply of humanity.

You are not thief.
Not man.
Not woman.
Vaguely human.

Christopher Michael

And *rapist*
is too large a word

to describe someone so tiny.

THE GRAVITY OF PITY

TRUTH: I have 5 inches of uneven dermis across my neck that has forgotten how to look like the rest of me.

FACT: I have a scar

STORY: In 1992 a psychiatric patient escapes the plush leather bracelets gifted to him by ER staff. They were complimentary with his bed like chocolate on a hotel pillow.

The patient quickly befriends a scalpel, the evil twin of butter knife. Like a long lost big brother who often confuses hugs with the latest wrestling move he embraces me from behind. Submerged in full-fledged illusion he was Perseus and I was the Medusa or maybe he was Hercules and I was Cerberus or one of the many heads of the hydra or he Beowulf and I was the dragon he'd been hunting.

His blade laid at the altar of my jugular. I never thought I would be anyone's ram in the bush. Whatever his schizophrenic fueled motivation I was trained to not lose my head in a crisis and he was determined to test my skills or ruin my day.

Before I could be rescued by my fellow gods of Mt. Olympus, Mr. Perseus-Beowulf-Hercules made his stand, and my neck was the ground (sand) he drew his line on (in).

I love this story because it makes me sound like the badass that I am.
But being a poet,
a man,
and a Texan,
I may have embellished
a bit.

SCAR? Fact
HOSPITAL? Truth
EMERGENCY ROOM? Operating Room
CRAZY PATIENT? MY doctor, who professionally, perhaps lovingly, but more likely cold and calculatingly removed the cancer that occupied my neck like a democratic-republic army looking for oil-freedom in the desert of my body. The cancer was so invasive that it

Christopher Michael

encroached my vocal chords as if to silence me like politically sensitive poets squelching freedom of speech. Irony: My doctor too was trying to create a safe space.

Perhaps I was nature's failed evolutionary experiment but I am not ashamed of the cancer I had. I am proud to know that when unwillingly thrust into the field of battle I fought and won. I endured botched follow-up care, causing cancer to spread to chest. I survived radiation treatment so potent, nurses weren't allowed in my room. I had to piss in a lead box and my nuclear spill classified vomit was left on the floor till I was strong enough to clean it up myself.

NOTE TO SELF: Add "hazardous waste management" to resume.

So, I lied.

I lie because people can't handle it. Their solace is a bigger burden than cancer. Their sympathy translates to pity, and pity carries so much weight it makes me weak. I am not strong enough to carry the weight of your sad eyes.

Don't pity me.
I don't want the gravity of your empathy.
Dap me.
Congratulate me.
I survived.

I survived like I drop kicked that psychotic motherfucker in the nuts before his blade dug a hole deeper than I could crawl out of.

By blade, I mean surgery.

By psychotic motherfucker, I mean cancer.

By survived, I mean I WON!

And you don't pity winners!!

JOB APPLICATION

HI.

My Name is Christopher Michael silkysmoothpenz October Brown

My government name? 002-91-1972

Oh, cause having a social security number implies that I may one day get social security. Calling it my government name is more accurate.

I was born right on time,

I write to time I slam.

Well, I expect to be paid what I am worth plus a percentage of your profits. I know in reality, I'll make 23 cents to the dollar more than the woman in the lobby who interviews after me.

Shit, maybe it will be cheaper to hire her.

Shit, I always talk myself out of good things.

My last girlfriend was a good thing.

The one before her was a good thing.

I married a good thing.

She left 'cause I did poetry. I talk too much.

Education?

I have a 4.0 in my nursing program.

I am fluent in bullshit, spoken word, slam and talking myself out of good things.

I hate my current job but I don't talk about it,

They pay me too much

it's a good thing.

Selective service?

Yes, I am a combat veteran and the thoughts of suicide are completely under control.

Employment?

I've worked as a player, a hustler.

I was not good at hustling so I quit.

I've worked as a two-timing asshole,

I was good at that, so I quit.

Oh!

I am a SlamMaster I love that.

Christopher Michael

I am the Vice President of Poetry Slam Incorporated a National Non-Profit.
I don't know if I'm good at that.
Inkera tolerates me, so I don't talk in meetings.
Oh, and I've been working as a good man,
a kind man,
I don't know if I'm good at that.
I'm a good father.
I've been one for 25 years.
They are black.
They are alive,
So, I guess I'm good at that.
I cannot quit.

Yes.
I do have one question.
Your form says "USE BLACK INK".
I am ink.
I am black.
My people are used to being used.
Can I have the job sir?

This poem was written as a challenge at the 2016 National Poetry Slam, Slam Master Slam. In the final round I was given a blank job application and ten minutes to write a poem. I won the slam ☺

PHUQS TO GIVE

So, I went to MegaSupaMart 'cause they
always have low low prices and when you're
running short and desperate you have to do
what you have to do. You try not to think
about their insane profits and low paid
employees. You push out the possibility the
hands that made what you need might be
barely older than two.

Aisle two, freezer section to extend their
preservation, eyes big, jaw dropped, mouth
watered. Breath yanked from chest as a
sacrifice for this box of beauty. A full
package of factory sealed exactly what I
need. Just touching the container made the
knots in my back and neck release their
gorilla-like grip. Anxiety subsides as waves
of peace magically seep through the seams.

So happy to have them, I refused to self-
checkout, 'cause I want to smile at someone
on my way out. Maybe bless them with one. In
line, completely forgiving the last person
on earth making their purchase with paper
check 'cause I, had what I needed. Made it
to check out with capitalvisa 1.5% cash
back; I was back.

Walked to the door, greeter checked receipt
with the corners of his mouth curled to the

Christopher Michael

heavens mimicking my own happiness. I now
have a fresh frozen set of Phuqs.
Finally fueled, I now have more Phuqs to
give cause TODAY, I'm gonna need to give a
Phuq to deal with people, life and adulting.
I can now walk into my place of employment
without choking the Phuq out of some one
'cause I now had my own.

Peers, subordinates and superiors at ease
with my smile 'cause clearly, I got what I
need. I offered up my full hands "See, this
is what the Phuq I was talking about." I had
enough for everyone, and I was in a sharing
mood.

Here's a phuq for you,
                              a phuq for you,
          phuq for you,
                    Phuq you!
                    PHUQ you!
               and PHUQ YOU TOO.

What the Phuq are you doing?

Phuqs are like puppies they need to be
tamed.

Get the Phuq off of there.

Calm the Phuq down.

Ok sit the Phuq down.

25

Now please shut the Phuq up.

Sssssshhhhh let it be. Don't get Phuqed up

You people are out of Phuqing control!

I walk in every morning, praying I can make
it to the end of the day alive, un-
incarcerated and still employed with just a
few left, 'til one day I can get the Phuq
out of there.

Christopher Michael

FAKERY

Regarding the people who rub you the wrong way and you're not sure why.

Your gut tells you something is wrong. You don't want to feel this. You want to flip the switch but your irritation with them is an intangible itch, a button you can't quite put your finger on.

You see fabricated emotional fits punctuated with tears that are counterfeit. They are imposters with simulated emotions you don't believe in them. They are 2Pac's hologram, a fabricated echo of truth. They are a poorly skilled actor cast in a reality show scripted by someone with no real-life experience.

You imagine that on a hot Texas day you can see the fake bubbling up through their pores a mockery of a real person glistening on their skin.

Maybe their sweat is fake. Maybe their pores are pretend.

Maybe the muscles that move their bones are bogus.

Maybe the piece of meat in the middle of their torso that forces air across the vocal chords shaped by lying lips is only as tangible as... freedom. Maybe the only real thing about them is the unexplainable discomfort felt when they are in a room. No, they haven't hurt you, wronged you or disrespected you (that you know of).

You just don't like them.

I JUST.

       DON'T.

              LIKE.

                    YOU.

Christopher Michael

– II –
Political Stuff

hai·ku
俳句

Cop used ebony colored gun
kills ebony man.
Black on black crime?

Christopher Michael

GLASS HOUSE

Hi my name is Christopher.
I say good morning to the sunrise
I get giddy over sunsets.
I love Grey's Anatomy
I watch lifetime on Sundays (sometimes).
I don't like football or basketball (At all).
I often put the toilet seat down and I've found,
men are disgusting.
Icky even
and I think I might be a lesbian.

I have more shoes than closet space.
It seems I like pretty colors and shiny things.
I use the word fabulous 'cause I think the word fabulous is well
fabulous.
I carry a man bag (back pack) not to be confused with a purse.
My chosen profession and field of work, Nurse.
I cry when people smile after I've chased away their hurt.
And I might be a lesbian.

How could I not be a lesbian?
Though I've no complaints from ladies about my strokin'em
I'd much rather be lickin'em than pokin'em.

I have no interest in relations with a man
that has no place in this discussion
as I said before I find men disgusting.
So I know I'm not gay
cause I know that I know
I only go one way.

31

So, if I were to wake as a woman one day brandishing tit and clit.
(My apologies ladies, I should say "breast and vagina.")
I wouldn't get out of bed.
Not out of fear,
embarrassment
or some type of dread
but because I would be busy,
um doing things.
Like cleaning,
vigorously,
over and over
It's time to face reality.
I am a lesbian trapped in the body,
of a very beautiful man,
Damn!

Problem is,
I haven't quite reasoned or reconciled this ridiculous reality
with my spiritual and cultural disagreements with
homosexuality.
Then again
isn't masturbation a form of homosexuality.

I often struggle with this inner conflict.
Not to have or not have a dick. (I'm sorry ladies a "penis.")
I love my penis
it's low maintenance,
I mean,
it's easy to clean.

I'm talking about the struggle between what I view as wrong
versus seeing two friends
in love
and actually getting along.
How do I resolve righteousness vs. wrongness vs.
happiness?

Christopher Michael

I am a bible believing Christian, life-long
and the bible clearly states that gay is wrong.
But then again
so is adultery
lying
stealing
and killing
and we've mastered those sins so far.
So I'm learning to love people for who they are.

Corinthians says
of faith,
hope
and love,
love is the greatest.

Peter said
above everything be excited in your love for one another
'cause it covers a multitude of sin.
If you don't love
you don't know God
cause God is love.

How could I possibly know the God in me is true,
if there's not even enough of him
in me,
to love you?

Hi,
My name is Christopher and I,
am learning.

MR. BULLET GOES TO WORK
Or
Mr. Bullet Takes A Life
Or
Mr. Bullet Says

Hey little nigga boy.
Hey thug.
Hey convict and future convict.
Hey dark truth veiled in hoodie,
ugly fact of American History,
forgotten contributor to the world.
Hey black girl with no name and no voice.

Mr. Bullet says;

Hey 60-year-old black boy!
Breaking into his own car,
in his own driveway.
Hey black boy, black girl!
Suspiciously sleeping in their car.
Hey black boy.
Aggressively reaching for his driver's license.
Hey you! In Wal-Mart, bout to buy toy gun!
Trigger warning.
Hey black folks, yawl done churchin', yawl
finished praying? Is Bible study over?
Hey little black boy,
I got another 40 friends that wanna come to
your wedding, maybe we can do some shots.

Mr. Bullet says;

34

Christopher Michael

You think you're fast little black boy!
You ain't fast!
You ain't no Jesse Owens,
you ain't no Florence Griffith-Joyner,
you ain't no Hussein Bolt you ain't fast.
Dying in your 20s, that's fast.
Dying before graduation, that's fast.
Dying at 12, wooooo that's fast.

!!!BOY!!!!

I'm 5 times faster than that BB gun laying
beside your body.

Damn you taste good.

I didn't expect your entrails to be so warm.
Is this why sharks followed slave ships through
the middle passage? Is this why flames loved to
picnic feast on your flesh? I almost feel sorry
for the noose that only gets to nibble on your
neck. On the way in, I just saw another black
silhouette. I thought this was practice. Little
nigga boy only 3/5 as valuable as white paper
targets but twice as tasty.

Why you got yo hands in the air?
You got questions?
You wanna know how fast I am.

On average,
I travel at 2,500 feet per second (around 1,700 mph).
That is to say,

you'd have to have been on the one-hundred-
and-fifty-yard line
for a hope
of a chance,
BUT YOU AIN'T!
THIS AIN'T THE MATRIX!
YOU CAN'T DODGE ME!
I BROKE THE SOUND BARRIER TWICE ON THE
WAY TO BREAKING YOUR BODY BOY!

Hey black girl. I'll get the city to pay your
family millions if you'll just let me inside of
you.

Mr. Bullet says;

I was made to make a good entrance
but my exits are much bigger.
Young boys don't know nothing bout blowing
nobody's back out,
once the trigger's pulled
I won't back out.
Cock,
   click,

   BANG!

      black
         out!

Christopher Michael

ZOMBIES SWARM

We are born zombie.
We live life walking dead.
Born in 3/5 a flesh only 2/5 from having an equal life.

We walk in black flesh.
Seen as the color of decay and death.

There is a war to destroy my people because our culture
spreads. A virus infecting the children of the privileged living,
they want to become us. They are seduced by the rhythm and
poetry of our moaning. They cook themselves to death under
the blaze of the sun they love our hew, man but they fear us.
They are necrophobes fighting to keep their people from
becoming necromancers and their daughters from turning into
necrophelliacs.

The soldiers of our extinction ride chariots with markings of
white over black, white separating black. They divide us. They
hunt us. They are experts in the art of provocation. Tailgating
into an illegal turn, 'til they turn nothing into something into
probable cause so they can light you up. So, they can noose
our Sandra Bland taste out of their mouths.

We seem to make some sick, as if the thick of our lips whispers
some pending ivory apocalypse. Maybe our skin is the dark
days that they fear. Maybe our foretelling is in a lost chapter of
revelations and only police have a copy. #blackdeathsmatter

So, they exterminate us one by one, but we keep walking, arms
outstretched as if begging for help. They are trying to un-
animate us. We are the characters they are constantly trying to
assassinate. Like bullets to our Malcolms and Martins they
shoot us in the head. The best way to kill a zombie is to take out
the head, but we keep marching, voices moaning but unheard.

Like Mindless zombies, we swarm the streets… Like

37

BEES SWARM

Like angry bees with no stingers we swarm the streets.

Something happened.

I'm not sure which something it is but something is always happening and now we are angry. We are outraged. We are hurt. We are mortified. We swarm.

We buzzed with anticipation of judgments reached, it was not the nectar we wanted. Our honey is now tainted we will swarm. We will descend upon our own hive and destroy it utterly. We will show the entire world that we are not to be trifled with. Give the verdict we want or we will destroy the flowers that support us. We trample over the very thing that keeps our hive in place we will chop down our tree.

We will not allow the bear to spill anymore of our honey. So we will destroy the nest before they get a chance to touch us again. We will not target the bear that threatens our home, we will target the trees that hold up the hive and the flowers that provide the nectar, we will swarm like they killed another queen.

How dare you; we swarm.

Irony: The planet's bees are slowly disappearing.

Christopher Michael

EYE AM HERE FOR YOU

Hey!
Excuse me!
Before you go to the union can you at least take me
out of the box? Yes, me, eye'm your brand-new body
cam.

Eye am here to protect you and keep you out of
trouble. Let me be your eyewitness and tell your
truth sir. I can exonerate you! Eye'll be like the
all-seeing eye on your chest. There's one on the
dollar, why not one on you?

Between you and eye, what happened to Sandra Bland?
See?

That's exactly what eye'm talking about. Eye know
he made a good call and if eye was there eye could
have cut away the cold commercial, cash-counting
cataract of the media. Eye would have highlighted
all the contempt and anger on her face, every
little wrinkle in her brow as she got out of place.
Eye could have shown the world what he saw, her
imminent threat to safety would have been obvious
and eye...

Just look at me as the next evolutionary step of
the dash cam.

Picture this: When you're chasing down some perp or
when you're breathing all heavy from the adrenaline
rush. Eye'll be there tapping you on your chest,
that gentle reminder. Eye can be like: *"Look they
put up their hands. Their palms are white. It's
like a flag of surrender. They're just like you.
You can almost see yourself in their empty hands."*

39

We can avoid all that #handsupdontshoot bullshit.
When you try to tell them it didn't happen. Eye can
prove it.

Don't let these, civilian, Ron Howard, JJ Abrams,
Spike Lee wannabes tell your story with their lame
ass cell phones. They just want YouTube hits. Let
me be your third eye and bring enlightenment upon
the jury for you. Eye'm your exhibit A. With me you
won't need exhibit D, C, OR B.

Look. As a lifelong member of the Public Eye Big
Brothers of America Union, eye don't understand why
you won't let me watch them with you, for you.

We watch trains and turn stiles, convenience
stores, elevators, taxicabs and airports. Eye went
to school with dudes who stare into space. The
block is hot and we got the watch on lock.

Eye'm not even trying to watch you. Just keep an
eye on things for you and attest to those moments
when the public disrespects you or threatens you
with they hands and suspicious movements.

Eye mean what's the big deal. My cousin Miles is
watching traffic, and his brother Standly is
hawking on the corner taking pics of folks running
red lights.

My sister Penny is at the bank making sure the
teller don't steal no money. Why can't eye roll
with you so eye can testify FOR you when you have
to kill somebody.

Eye just want to be your friend.

Christopher Michael

In case no one has told you lately. Thank you for putting your life on the line every day for us. I know your job is dangerous and I appreciate you.

Eye know it's kinda creepy and eye certainly don't want anybody watching me while eye do my job watching.

Looky here, looky here! They got the taxpayers to pay for me as a life saving measure and tool for accountability, but in reality, sssshhhh, eye'm here to protect your pension.

Look at me as an artist painting your story. Eye am Picasso the way eye process these photons into digital dots, the facts of your truth, eye am here for you.

Eye just wanna watch. ☺ See if you're naughty or nice.

Santa clause ain't got shit on me!!

So, pick me up.

    Put me on.

        Now let's go serve and protect.

THE OCTOPUS MENACE

The octopus' genome is so foreign scientists consider it alien. So, why don't we hunt it down? Why are we not punishing it for its differences? Why aren't we patrolling and policing the oceans to keep ourselves safe from these spineless aquatic thugs?

They are experts in the art of camouflage like sacrificing beards and locks. Then dawning ties to lynch... blend in with corporate America.

Exceptionally intelligent but can't pass information from one generation to the next, like a black Mother, it kills itself watching the nest.

But where is the father?
Like too many black men
black boys,
having children
they don't stick around,
'cause no one stuck around for them,
'cause no one stuck around for them.

What do they have suction cups for if not to stick around?
Maybe if men had suction cups they'd be more willing to stick around.

Thank God for short life spans and weak community.

Community!

Walls!

Why aren't we building walls around these oceans?
What if they crawl out and steal all the jobs we don't want?

Christopher Michael

Just imagine, all those arms reaching out for assistance and entitlements. Next, they'll all want equal opportunity and justice.

We need to stop this venomous creature before it spits more black ink.

The octopus is a clear and present danger!

Stop wasting money, building schools to teach them!

We need more prisons!

HERBICIDAL MANIAC

My nose,
my ears,
my eyes,
my throat,
my whole face stands in protest against the onslaught of
reproductive dust spewed into the air by the local vegetation as
if they think my sinuses are a willing participant in this shrub on
shrub orgy.

I'd wave the white flag of my eyes but they're obscured by the
reddening effects of plant procreation. Can they not see the
snot marching from my nostrils demanding redress? Do they
not hear the silent cries of histamine as they peacefully sit in my
mucous membranes swollen to closure as if saying, *"We will no
longer supply you trees with the carbon dioxide you need to
breathe."* Forgetting that I TOO NEED TO BREATHE!

I'd love nothing more than to pluck every,
pollen polluting plant,
flower and weed,
we need a Round Up!

I'm one sneeze away from becoming a herbicidal maniac, gladly
chopping down every cedar tree constantly accosting me with
its stray ejaculate. Quite literally phuqing me in the face!

and WHY DOES MY THROAT ITCH?

I don't go green,
but if I did
I wouldn't swallow.
So why are you in my mouth?

Or maybe…

44

Christopher Michael

Maybe, these are secret service mold spores tapping my tongue like some misguided patriot act 'cause they know my thoughts conspire into dreams of the sweet sounds of swinging axes, gasoline powered chain saws and the angelic baritone sound of timbeeerrrr.

But alas, they provide me with services I seemingly can't live without, like oxygen. In exchange every few months despite my monetary offerings to pharmaceutical companies to stave off the unwanted nasal invasion, I gotta take what they're giving. Right up the nose!

To ensure that the reader can relate to my pain I shall endeavor to delve in metaphor to highlight my affliction.

It's like paying taxes. I appreciate the perceived freedoms, roads and military security but no matter how much they take from my check no matter what valuable service they provide I still feel violated with little recourse available to me.

It's no coincidence that allergy season coincides with...

!!!Tax Season!!!

I'm not overreacting,
these trees are over pollinating
like a botanical prom night.

Pouring pollen into the air like lobbyists pour cash into Capitol Hill, Pollenticians forcing pork into every bill.

These trees are corrupt! They say they're all about solar energy, recycling and cleaning the environment but year after year they phuq you, right in your face!

BACON

I love bacon so much!
I keep a small can of it in my back pocket
in case my blood pork level gets too low,
I can stuff a pinch of bacon bits between cheek and gum.

This isn't high blood pressure!
THIS! is an excessive buildup of joy I'm about ready to bust!

The best part of waking up ♫ ...

Imagine,
a small vial of powdered bacon,
poured on to ceramic plate.
Then cut in lines with a thin crispy slice of bacon.
With another piece of bacon rolled into a straw

        <sniiiiiiiffff>
        WHOA!!! That's good shit!
Uncut pure USDA CHOICE!
It smells so good.

How do you speak the name of GAWD without the sweet aroma
of bacon in your lungs?

Haiku Interlude:
Adam and Eve ate
from the tree of knowledge learned
how to cook BACON!!!

How could non-bacon eaters even be children of God?
Wait!
Excuse me?
You wanna transition?
From bacon to turkey bacon?

        Bullshit!

46

Christopher Michael

No one's born that way.

Shot by the police on a random traffic stop? *Don't disrespect the bacon!*

People who don't eat bacon should have separate bathrooms. They should not be allowed to marry or adopt children. How do you raise a child in that way of life? We should build a wall around all the non-bacon eaters, and make them pay for it. They should get 23 cents less an hour than the rest of us.

How can they have equality…

                    IF THEY'RE DIFFERENT???

Is this not

the most ridiculous mess you've ever heard?

Eat what you wanna eat!

Do what you wanna do!

Love who you wanna love!

Stand for the flag!

Sit for the flag!

Just don't hurt nobody…

                    And do it with a side of bacon.

Christopher Michael

SHE'S TOO BLACK

She had to have been honored when she was elevated to the level of social media specimen or perhaps lowered to a two-dimensional meme. Clad in bra and panties *or maybe summer bikini,* light green contrasting the mountain of melanin decorating her skin with the title…

"She's Too **Black**"

Yo this bitch is so **black**…

She was so **black,** I lost myself looking into her skin.
She was so **black,** the sweat glistening on her arms looked like a starry night
unmolested by gentrified city lights,
like the universe man has been dreaming of exploring.

Black as the back drop of nebulas birthing stars
you can almost see galaxies pressing into each other
like long lost lovers reunited.

She was **black** enough to conceal frightened travelers on the Underground Railroad.
She was **black** like before God spoke.
Black like the eclipse
that scared the shit
out of cave dwellers
before they pillaged Egypt for math and medicine.

Too **black** for you to understand what you're looking at.
Too **black** for boys to behold.
Yo bro you must be the bitch
'cause dogs can't see color.
Hard to appreciate her beauty
when your ignorance, can only see **black** or **white**.

49

The Flash & America: A Poetic Indictment

Christopher Michael

Nuclear Orange

310 Brown Street Publishing

January 7th, 2017

Overview

The Flash is arguably the fastest man on Earth. That is if he wasn't a fabricated story to sell things to children. America is arguably the greatest nation on Earth. That is if it wasn't a fabricated story to sell things to adults.

Comparison

The Flash, the fastest man alive, endowed with super speed, after a freak lightning strike while being randomly covered in a concoction of chemicals. I wonder what would happen to fish in the Gulf if they, were struck by lightning.

The Flash once ran across the universe in less than a Planck instant He tapped into the kinetic energy from every person on earth as they all ran as fast as they could at the exact, same time (Morrison & Millar, 1998). You can't even get together to vote or agree on sensible legislation.

51

If you, were struck by lightning after being doused with chemicals, you would die. Well, first your heart would stop. Then you'd burst into flames. Then you would die. You, however, you will not wake up with the ability to outrun your troubles or erase the horrors hidden in your foundation.

Wishful Thinking

Apparently, the flash is fast enough to cross time (Geoff, 2011). It doesn't matter how fast you run ~~nigga~~, America, you will never be the Flash, Jay Garrick, Barry Allen, Walley West, you can't change time. You can't outrun your past. You can't undo the bullshit. I wish our crumbling school system could teach ~~black lives~~ all lives how to outrun bloodhounds thirsty for dark flesh oddly shaped like bullets. You can't even outrun the NRA's grip on Congress let alone outrun the club shooting yesterday or the church shooting the other

Christopher Michael

day, or the school shooting last week, or the
school shooting last month or the school shooting
the month before last, or blue lines bullet
lynching ~~Ebony~~ bodies that one time or the other
time or the time before last or the time before
that or all the other times homicide was justified.

I get it! You're being weighed down, so you
can't run, probably 'cause of probable cause or
stop and frisk or manifest destiny or Jim Crow,
reservations, gentrification, indigenous
extermination, crack, internment camps, or forced
labor in cotton fields, you're not fast enough.
Hell, half of you is trying to rise again like a
Confederate zombie apocalypse, blindly walking dead
trying to be great again. How can you outrun the
past when you're still living in it?

Reality Check

Through a process called quantum tunneling, The Flash can vibrate himself at a resonance that allows him to phase through solid objects. You can't even get through to the American people let alone a brick wall. There are so many to blame, corporate media with conflicting interest, social media with opinions devoid of facts, and a lazy populace with a questionable desire to do research.

Science

If! The Flash could move as fast as the comic books portray, he would nuke the planet. Atoms in the atmosphere couldn't move out of his way fast enough so they would split and mushroom explode all over the place. So, through magic, the speed force or poetic license, atoms just don't get in his way.

Since there is no speed force, and your poetic license expired shortly after the writing of the

Christopher Michael

constitution, and you refuse to acknowledge black girl magic or the magic at the end of rainbows I guess you won't be moving anything out of the way like: racism, prejudice, inequality, hypocrisy, conservative agendas, or liberal agendas. Your politicians are so stuck on agendas, they are always refusing to move shit out of the way preferring to split in half, chain reaction explode all over the American voter / couch potato / Monday morning quarterback.

Summary

Justice League? You can't have a league without unity and justice has a price tag. You can, however, outrun the truth with your power to rewrite history. America, you are no Flash. You are hardly even the land you promised you'd be.

Reference

Grant Morrison and Mark Millar (April–June 1998). *Flash*

(second series) #136–138, DC Comics

Johns, Geoff (w) (May-August 2011). *Flashpoint* 1-5 DC Comics

Christopher Michael

– III –
The Flash & Fireball
"Carrots"

hai·ku
俳句

I did not shower
cause I like the smell of you
all over my face.

I gave her roses.
She gave me tulips wet and
pressed against my face.

Christopher Michael

FEELING HER

I'm **feeling** the fact that the father forged the feminine figure to free fellas from frustration but the temptation to touch this tantalizing tart starts my stomach doing stunts I can't stand it I can't negate these nasty narrations these naughty notations that navigate my neurons **her** body's to blame when like a moth to the flame my mind migrates the marriage of this milky magnificent mocha complexion her physical perfection demands my affection behold this beauty that bounds by my eye my dain is doggled my drain is broggled my brain is boggled by the bounty of her breast I'm blessed just to be by her as if the bounty of her breast weren't enough you wouldn't believe the bricks you could bounce off her booty pure beauty I'm serious about the sexiness of this sultry siren even her sweat is sweet I think if I think another thought about those thick thighs oh my oh my why she so fly this hormone high is hell on my health hips highlighted by heaven's hands and have you seen her hair even her hands are heavenly inevitably my heart's gone halt I can't handle this oh hell have you seen her toe nails perfectly painted first time saw them damn near fainted even the way she licks her luscious lips leaves you longing to love her right she's tight you'd fight just to spend one night loving her right this cold cutie had the kinda curves a classic corvette couldn't corner. I could tell she wanted me by the size of her... smile so slowly I slinked up to this sexy sister obviously anxiously awaiting the arrival of what I have to offer. After a bold but brief oration of my opulent offer she offered me her hand, to talk to. Clearly she was uninterested in advances. In response to her rudeness I offered her some choice words like "have a good day ma'am I apologize for disturbing you."
Hey friend, young man, son, every smile is not an invitation.
Let her walk the street in peace.

SIN

What do you do when just a chance
of Her glance
has you climbing the walls?

Cell phone checks every 10 minutes looking for Her missed
calls, afraid to sleep at night 'cause you might fall,
for Her beauty,
Her smile,
Her laugh is the fine combustible powder in me that's ready to
explode
and at this point I'm as stable as a glass of nitro in the palm of
Parkinson's patient on a bumpy road
contemplating on trading today for tomorrow
trying to keep my emotions under control
I attempt to keep my distance
don't reveal your weakness says Shin Zu
so *I* refuse to expose my passion's short fuse
but just my luck
she's wearing Egyptian musk
and it was all the spark I needed to ignite my lust
but I must
keep my cool
there's rules
so no mention of names
just she the flame
and I pray my salvation is secure
cause at this rate I'm not getting in
so I continue to pretend
I'm not supposed to know the softness of Her lips
or the smoothness of Her skin
                          SIN
forbidden from finding the point where thighs end
and her fountain begins
can't open Her door and walk in

Christopher Michael

i don't resist temptation because it's right to do so
or wrong to give in
i resist temptation
cause it makes for a sweeter "SINce you're here
come on in"

casual conversation carries over to casual touch
but there's no such thing as casual touch
when you want something this much
so casually i move in
because at the moment
i don't see anything wrong
with tasting the lips of a really good friend
and it was an accident when my tongue slipped in

i could think of no reason
why not to run my fingers across Her body
like i was playing bass
in an all skin band
tickling Her keys 'cause nothing in the world matters
but Her in my hands
and the music i was about to play
had a tear of joy
running down Her thigh

and i'm thinking to myself

maybe we should stop

and i'm yelling at myself

but why?

i was close enough to feel Her heart
beating like a gemba drum
made my senses go numb
to hell with the consequences i just want some

alright
step beck
move away

61

don't give in
it's not too late to repent your sin

come on man you're a poet
hit Her with a smooth line

"hey look at the time
i'm supposed to be making some pies
for the church fundraiser"

anxiety has my chest all tight
but the remnants of **Her** aroma on my lips
made it easier to breathe

i inhale
and exhale
memories of stolen moments meditating on the echoes of **Her**
saying "Maybe We Should Stop… Please."

God must be thanked
because i showed some restraint
but if we meet again
Her clothes will not be my friend
we won't stop till we cum to the inevitable end.

Question:
So what do you do when just a chance of Her glance has you
climbing the walls? Cell phone checks every 10 minutes looking
for **_Her_** missed calls, afraid to sleep at night 'cause you might
fall,
into sin

Christopher Michael

THEORETICAL LOVE

I've had my eye on you longer than you could imagine.
My thoughts for you travel deeper than the Nautilus could
fathom. Imagine Stephen Hawking stalking his favorite
worm hole 'cause he knows if he could just get inside in an
instant he'd Slide across your Einstein-Rosen bridge and be
on the other side of ecstasy.

Imagine me walking on your moon, I may Neil but I'll
always be Armstrong by your side.

My heartbeats radio waves like the HAARP array strong
enough to alter weather patterns to brighten your day.

Let's meet in the crease as I fold time and space, like that
last love letter I sent you then we'll push the envelope of
what love could be.

77565

"BABY"

The sound rolls off her tongue like the last drop of water in a
barren wasteland
and I stand
ready to receive her with cupped hands
I'm not sure if it's always been a part of her regular vocabulary
but when she
says baby to me
it feels like she's never said it to anyone but me
it comforts me

Like a warm blanket in chilly room
fully immersed as if I was back in the womb
This may sound dumb
but, she makes a brother wanna suck his thumb
She makes me feel like it's ok to be vulnerable, open and
honest
She makes me feel like it's ok to be weak without losing the
strength of my hand
she makes me feel like a man
Baby dances on her lips mere seconds but it's more like hours
in a hot shower
after a stress filled day the sound consumes me with its warmth
raising the temperature of my body
just enough to separate me from the coldness of my reality

One of her babys makes my feel like I I fell in love for the first
time
multiplied 100 times
I'm

Lost in the thought of her saying baby it makes me weak
it makes me feel like my heart skipped a beat.
It makes me feel like my insides shifted
this is what it must be like to feel splifted

64

Christopher Michael

almost like being Holy Ghost lifted
Every letter and both syllables sneaks in to my ears and down
my spine
and for the briefest of time
I'm
two hundred and twenty-five pounds of quivering jello
Solid, tangible, visible, but just like jello
she sees right through me and with the softest touch she
passes right through
It's like my heart is that orange slice in the center she's trying to
get to
I don't always do
what she wants me to do
She uses that word like she's a jockey with a whip
And I'm her stallion chomping at the bit
She uses baby like some kind of Jedi mind trick
And I'm left dangling on her hook like a big mouth bass that just
took the bait
I can't wait to do whatever it is she wants me to do

She says it and it melts me
Like Obi Wan she persuades me
I swear she is the voice of heaven

It's too bad she wasn't there September 11th
That's when she should have used her power / what a more
useful way to wield her power

Baby don't fly in to that tower
Oh, George baby move faster we're under attack!
Baby wrong country don't bomb Iraq!
Baby find Bin Laden he's the problem!
Baby bring the troops home they don't wanna die for oil no
more!
We've made enough money lower gas prices stop gouging the
poor!
Stop the genocide in Darfur!
Baby, make the teachers stop sleeping with our babies!

Nuclear Orange

Prosecute those cops!
Being Black's not a crime he didn't deserve 43 shots!
Baby even if you think abortion's wrong it's not your decision
Baby you have more important things to do
who marries who
is none of your business!
Baby there's nothing patriotic about that act!
Baby that's illegal you can't do that!

BABY!!

If her Babys were mine I would share them with the...

No I wouldn't.

I'd keep them
for myself...

Christopher Michael

THE MUSE

She asked me to write her a poem.
I told her I don't do requests,
                                    besides my ink stopped flowing,
                my pens gone dry.
Her reply…
let me wet your Bic with the tip of my lips
girl's lips were – thick – lips beautiful mouth
3 times a lady she was a brick – house(d) – in her the hope of
another poem.
She wanted me to spit spoken about her out my mouth
                                            but I was too distracted
by what I could put in – hers – was beautiful.
Lips glossed like a shiny door
inviting me to ask for more.
And for the life of me
I don't know what the hell I did to earn the key.
Plaguing me
like a vulture perched on my pen is the poisoned pain of writer's
block   and dry Bic.
I found it acceptable to allow for the exchange of biochemical
electrical impulses between my left and right brain to explore
the possibility of the reality of letting her lips rewet my Bic tip but
left brain thought the right was wrong because realistically all of
this was just metaphor and hyperbole.
I really wish it was that easy
                                to breathe life into my
hands by wetting my Bic tip on those thick lips.
What the hell!
I gave it a try.
I let her wet the tip of my Bic
and before long my Bic was really…

really…

                wet.

I still
wasn't
writing.
Wait!
Something's
coming
to me

             AN EPIPHANY.

Maybe…
the best way for me to spit spoken is for me to drink straight
from the source.
I dipped my tongue in her well

           and with a whispered yell

like an old Kung Fu Master she tells me,
           *You'll know you've done it
right when you can tell me what my cervix – tastes like –* a
mouth full of warm wet metaphors. She left lingering on my lips
a delicious layer of alliteration. I think I've tasted the coveted
cradle of creation.
Oh my!   I'm creating!
Creating like she just sexed me unprotected
and left her seed in my mouth.

         My tongue is giving birth like
Adam's seed in Eve was purposed to trample on the head of
satan.   Her seed in me is why I've been waiting.
                 The
reason I wasn't creating

        is because my poems were still
gestating.

I drank until my pen was hard enough to chisel a poem on her
walls.

     You make me feel like a snake charmer

     the way your body coils up and out

Christopher Michael

of a basket of beauty
as if mesmerized by my words.

Your mistake
is not realizing that I
am the snake
utterly charmed by everything about you.

Your unending beauty is merely a thin layer of
icing on you   the triple layer chocolate cake.

Before a seed bears fruit
the roots must first
reach deep
in the depths of the death and decay of the dirt.

Then!

BLOSSOM

– IV –
The Blast
"Sun Rise"

hai·ku
俳句

She's not writing a haiku.
She's counting
the orgasms I gave her.

Drink

 I love the way she melts in my arms,
spills into my hands
so I drink.
Drink like my life depends on getting as much of
her in me as possible.

We be the perfect metaphor for infinity. Her in me
and me in her and we be one. Like the one puddle
she leaves in my mattress a reflecting pool so I
reflect.
        Like the reflection she leaves in my eyes a
blinding light burns brilliant her beautiful frame
to my brain.
        Then a touch,
A kiss
and we can't resist the kiss.

Imagine this,

Silk, satin and cashmere
warm, melting on your mouth.
Tongues dance to the drums
of a smooth heartbeat rhythm.
Arms wrapped round waist
pulling breast to chest.
Left hand caresses back like I was finally playing
that bass in the all skin band neck rest in right
hand.

So enamored
we touch fingers to face and lips
just to convince
the rest of the body we are actually enjoying
something as much
as this beautifully simple kiss.

72

Christopher Michael

I nuzzle neck and pause
to feel her life pulse past my lips.
Palms pay alms to arms
to position her right where I need her.

I delicately un-wrap my favorite piece of candy
mouth-watering wet I'm ready to eat.

I… recommend you purchase Persona Non Grata pg.75
if you would like to read the rest of *Drink* ©2015.
Go to www.mrmichael310.com

LOVE & LAND MINES

A good woman
is like a land mine.
Once you step in that kind of love
you know walking away
would kill you,

blowing your world in more pieces
than the potter
could possibly
completely pick up
and put back together.

Once you break something as fragile as a heart
you can never find all the pieces
and there is no glue
that can hide all the fractures.

Christopher Michael

If you are the skeleton in someone's closet, step into the light and let your beautiful bones be bleached by the cleansing rays of the son... of the sun. Cover your bones with the meat of self-respect. With new muscle comes new strength. Walk. If they can't walk with you in the light then they will despise you in the dark. Walk. Walk until you find you. You will be the one with your head held high and your chest out. You are nobody's shame. You deserve the best, simply because you are loved by HIM. Blossoms don't bloom in the shadow of shame. The only thing that should be poked in your heart is the perfectly rounded stem of your favorite flowers tended by the one Gardner appointed by HIM who is not afraid of your dirt. He will understand that shit and death make life grow. If they are ashamed of your shit, then let them go.

What did the left butt cheek say to the right butt cheek?

If we stick together we can stop this shit.

**Never trust anyone
who doesn't appreciate
a good shit joke.**

DOOKIE MAN

Thousands of comedians have made their mark with jokes that pertain to me. In polite company, you try to refrain from me. Pharmaceutical companies have made millions trying to contain me.

For I am that growl that howls when you smile trying to hide it.
Keep me from open flame I'll ignite it.
A room full of friends I'll divide it.
I'm too wet and loose to contain so don't try to fight it.

I am that one for Pepto you are yearning.
I am the one that has your booty burning.
I am the fish filet you had at eight.
I am those greasy fries you ate too late.
I am the chitlins you didn't clean.
I am the one that made you dookie green.

I am the one that made you vomit.
I am the explosive diarrhea that lit your ass up like a comet.
I am the heartburn that got you clutching your chest.
I am that stale ass burp that has you holding your breath.
I am the chili pepper that you regret sir,
dammit it's just too late for Alka-Seltzer.
I am the shrimp and sushi salad you thought might be bad,
now I'm the lingering odor in the back of the cab
and you knew something was wrong.
Now I'm that long drive home.

And when you get there.
I am the one that has you at home
on the throne
rocking back and forth like windshield wipers.
I am that one that has grown men
wishing they could still wear diapers.

I am that funk,

Christopher Michael

that fart
that warning sign and you tried to play ignorant,
now everyone knows you're lactose intolerant.

I had you running from too much Hershey and Nestle,
with just one push I killed Elvis Presley.
I am that one that has you saying damn
that intense pressure in my gut.
I am that traffic jam
when that turtle head is poking out your butt.

I am that crippling cramp that causes bodies to buckle
and bellies to bend.
I am the hot winds
that spends
fogging contact lens
and choking friends.

I am the one that makes bellies grumble,
when you race for the toilet I make you stumble.
I am that warm sensation down your thigh that makes you humble.

You can try to slow me down with your Ka Oh Pec Tate
but I just can't be stopped.
I can move bowels.
For I am
I am
I am
Da SHIT!

BELLY BUTTONS

My belly button
is the evidence
of the vacuum in my soul
created when seeing her leave
the scene without me
sucks the life out of me.

She is my breath I keep running out of
I'm running trying to catch it
but I'm tired
and my feet hurt
from walking on eggshells.

Left out of breath
head barely above water
I'm out of my depth.

Christopher Michael

SEVERED FINGERS & HEAVY BAGS

With all the bags you have,
with everything that weighs you down,
why would you burden yourself with someone
else's?

Why are you carrying the hate of someone who
never crossed you
for a friend who let it go a handful of blue moons
ago?
You must be so tired.
That bag you carry is like a black hole
infinitely heavy
but infinitely hollow.
Let it go!

How do you touch anyone with those calloused
hands...
and enjoy it?

The weight of bag straps have elongated your
fingers making it easier for you to point the
blame
fueled by the half truth
completely skewed perception
of what you think happened.

'Til the gravity of those bags severed your finger
tips.
You hold on to those bags even though it's
pointless.

I don't know you
or care enough about you to have this
conversation face to face
but I hope this speech will reach someone I do
care about
and don't know they're in danger of severed
finger tips.
Hopefully they
will get the
point
of this
!!!
!!
!

.

Christopher Michael

– IVSS –
The Looking Glass

Self-Reflection

hai·ku
俳句

Large cool glass filled with
sweet humility. I still
can't swallow my pride.

He the player
true ladies' man
heart unprotected
he's out of ribs.

Penis on outside
makes room for emotions
he hides on the inside.

Till the ground,
water the seed,
reap what you sow.
I pray for crop failure.

Christopher Michael

This is the part where I would put all the stupid things I did in the relationship, but I didn't write any poems about that, so we'll skip this section.

– V –
The Firestorm
"Sun Set"

hai·ku
俳句

She should have won an
Olympic Gold Medal in
Conclusion Jumping.

The common factor in the demise
of all your relationships...
you

She is phuqing incredible
I wish my name was incredible

The Stench

Upon initial contact with olfactory bulbs, deceptively sweet particles trigger a response in grey matter causing nostrils to spread wide recreating prom night 1991.

Then mere seconds later the bait and switch. There's a distinct aromatic undertone that forces primal instinct to take over.

Body shutters,
nostrils close,
hand over nose,
for emergency backup
lips clenched to block the stench,
all before my conscious mind realizes
the 1944 Normandy style nasal invasion has begun.

The noisomeness
can easily be compared to the aroma of infected fecal matter,
marinated in rancid milk
after the electricity
has failed to provide the refrigerator with adequate fuel
to keep the particles under control.
This is akin to the reaction had...

when you start bringing up old shit!

The entirety of *The Stench* ©2015, can be read in Persona Non Grata pg.47 www.mrmichael310.com

Christopher Michael

RAZORS & REGRETS

She sharpens Her tongue with my mistakes
like a razor she cuts a reminder of my sins against Her,
into my ear.

I'm trying not to sweat Her
I wear parkas and sweaters
in the Texas summers to muffle the sounds
of my heart calling out for Her.

Anger strengthens my bones
but hatred is a weight too heavy for me to hold.

My crimes
constantly weighed against my present
and future pain
no forgiveness for fools.
My mistakes have made my emotions,
null,
void,
invalid
and inconsequential.

I laid down my pride
so I could be the mat she needs to clean her feet
of the dirt I left.
But it's time
for me to reclaim my pride and be a man.
No more walking on me
my name is Michael not Mat
this is where I make my stand.

Nuclear Orange

THE RELAPSE

There is not much difference between drug addiction
and love.

When that thing,
when that person
you are addicted to,
in love with,
is out of reach you feel sick,
you feel empty,
you are irrational,
willing to do anything,
will do anything
to have another hit.

Doesn't matter how much it hurts,
how much friends attempt to intervene,
you can't think straight.
How can you,
when all you see
are the curves of their silhouette
in your mind's eye?

You have no desire
to think beyond the mushroom cloud of recollections
that fog your grey matter.
The chemistry of your brain rewritten
and now you are hopelessly hooked.
Every memory of them is bait for you to bite.

Why does this hurt so good?

Christopher Michael

You forget all the bad times
as if your mind hides the trauma.
All you know is the rush
and the balance
of a steady supply.

When you get another hit,
when you get, them back
the world seems right
(for now)
even though this thing,
even though this person
is slowly killing you.

You finally break free of the grip.
Weeks,
          months
                    years go by
                              and you
                                        are free!!

Until you see them,
                    taste them,
                              have them again

                    you

                    have Relapsed.

LOVE TURNS COWARDS INTO LIONS

It took an entire trip of poisoned poppy seed romping, winged-monkey fighting, and wicked witch killing for me to finally muster the courage to tell you how I feel. But by the time I could rumble the roar out of my belly your heels were clicked together two and a half times.

Maybe if I roar hard enough the heat from my lungs will clash with the cold air of the tin man's empty chest and create a low-pressure system and tornado that will take me back to you.

I'm no coward
I never was
I'm just shy.

The only thing I'm afraid of
is being without you.

The scarecrow ain't smart enough to know a good thing when he sees it. There's nothing you can do to put a heart inside a piece of tin but I have one, and it beats your name like an award-winning concerto, an opus of love. I may not be a man but this flesh and blood grows warm with thoughts of your love.

Mr. Wizard, I've changed my mind.
I don't want courage
I want Her.

Christopher Michael

– VI –
The Fall Out
"Camp Fires"

hai·ku
hai·ku

俳句

He is drunk,
aims nuclear tipped arrows.
That demon of lust,
Cupid.

Her name is misery
and I have grown tired
of her company.

Be thankful for the shrapnel in your chest.
At least you dodged the bullet.

WANTED: A good woman
I can run from, when she starts
treating me well.

Madison Thomas

Christopher Michael

NUCLEAR ORANGE

Carrots,

     sunrises,

          sunsets,

              and campfires.

There's something about the color orange that stops me in my tracks. Needless to say, it's my favorite color.

Cupid, has a warped sense of humor, he unites plutonium and dynamite. I'm not sure which of us was which, but we were a force and she was blowing my mind, explosions like the kind the universe was birthed from, I bet it was orange.

The first kiss, was like the click, of a land mine, the blast should have killed us, instead the heat of passion seared our flesh to one 'til separating was as painful as staying together. Holding on was easier than seeking the peace we both deserved like most civilized societies we sought freedom through war. Sadism comes in all shapes and sizes and we practiced pain like we studied at UT, full ride, scholarship. We know how to hurt 'cause hurting is as easy as being hurt.

We were a divine, dazzling disaster like a mushroom cloud. Inside our breathtaking billow of smoke was a beautiful shade of orange, I couldn't turn away. Alluring, powerful and completely destructive, like two atoms in a super collider slammed together at the speed of right! Wrong! Particles separate, releasing an energy this man could not understand or control.

We were supposed to be together but when you **im**properly sup**pose** you **im/pose**. Forcing pieces together even when they

93

almost fit, still requires some level of destruction from one or both pieces. Something has to be cut, crushed or severed.

Hearts break, heal, scar, resentment turns tumors I was just looking for some treatment and she was my chemotherapy but no one told me chemo kills good tissue along with the bad.

Every part of my body was lead lined except for my heart and my spine. I couldn't avoid the exposure. The radioactive residue from our relationship was sloughing off the skin of my self-respect. I tried to avoid the exposure but I couldn't let go, or look away blinded by the beautiful light of our explosion. How ironic is it that carrots are supposed to help improve your vision but I still wasn't seeing straight. Stumbling for cover but refusing to leave the battlefield. How do I apologize to the women I used as bomb shelters to hide from our fall out?

Cupid, the god of passionate love, lust, like flame. His arrow is nuclear tipped and he's dyslexic. We should have paid attention to the only God of love and he told me to duck.

We loved each other like flames but like campfires, they don't stop 'til there's nothing left to consume (or someone pees on you).

We were a defiant Nagasaki and Hiroshima embracing all the love America had to deliver. We exploded at the beginning and ending like the horizon of each day.

Carrots, sunsets, sunrises, campfires. There's something about the color orange that stops me in my tracks.

But so do landmines.

Christopher Michael

FIELD OF FLAMMABLE FANTASIES

I'm standing in a field of flammable fantasies and gasoline dreams desperately trying to rekindle a flame with a wet match that's already been used. Meaning: I'm going after something that ain't gonna happen, 'cause if it did, it would be nothing but destructive.

Query: What kind of farmer doesn't eat from his own field? Doesn't matter how much you give you have got to keep something for yourself. If not, you will starve in your own vacuum of emptiness.

Maybe I didn't dodge the bullet, but I'm walking away,
alive,
with a limp.
Not to brag, but the limp adds to the swag.

I loved Her so much I transed-my-form to carry Her.
Rolling out on bald tires I frequently lost my grip.

I've been in the kind of love that's left men on freeways
hoping for hugs by 18 wheels
but I considered who may miss me.
I'm glad those 18 wheels missed me.

My mistake
is I loved Her more than she had room to receive
cause he still had Her cup full,
so my love overflowed
onto another

I was the fool...

95

More times than I can count.

So many moments I sacrificed myself to the heat of our volcano.
Who wouldn't get addicted to that kind of passion?
But volcanoes have toxic gasses,
I thought it was love that was taking my breath away.

Does Cupid bother to read hearts before he takes aim?
Maybe mine was drunk.

I thought you were perfect.
You were beautiful
and everything I wanted.

I still think you're perfect.

Just not for me.

Christopher Michael

Fallout or Bomb Shelter

A **fallout shelter** is an enclosed space specially designed to protect occupants from radioactive debris or fallout resulting from a nuclear explosion. Many such shelters were constructed as civil defense measures during the Cold War.

During a nuclear explosion, matter vaporized in the resulting fireball is exposed to neutrons from the explosion, absorbs them, and becomes radioactive. When this material condenses in the rain, it forms dust and light sandy materials that resembles ground pumice. The fallout emits alpha and beta particles, as well as gamma rays.

Much of this highly radioactive material falls to earth, subjecting anything within the line of sight to radiation, becoming a significant hazard. A fallout shelter is designed to allow its occupants to minimize exposure to harmful fallout until radioactivity has decayed to a safer level.

Reference

Fallout shelter. (n.d.). In *Wikipedia*. Retrieved November 26, 2016, from https://en.wikipedia.org/wiki/Fallout_shelter

ZOMBIE LOSS

I've decided to remove your lower jaw
and not because you never stop talking
but because I'm afraid you might bite me
and infect me
with whatever virus that has you following me,
Mindlessly,
desperately
trying to feast on my heart.

I'm afraid of you.
I'm afraid if you don't devour all that I am
AND all that is left
what is in you
will get in me
and make me
want to consume someone as badly
as you try to take me in.

It's like
you've been doomed to this perpetual hunger
and you've caught my scent.
I panic at the prospect of being like that...

                                    Again.

I've decided to remove your arms,
because your embrace
terrifies me.
You hold on so tight.

Clearly
I'm penetrating the wrong part of your body
with the wrong weapon
because you keep coming.

Christopher Michael

I would shoot you
but I failed to properly prepare for this apocalypse
but I do got this bow and arrow that I ain't really good with.

I only seem to hit you in the heart
which we all know is completely ineffective
when dealing with your kind.
You only seem to come on stronger when I do,
you'd think this archery equipment was manufactured
by the cupids.

It's like no matter how much what I do
should kill you,
you keep coming back
even more animated than before
and no matter how fast and how far I run
when I turnaround
your arms are outstretched
reaching for me.

Maybe,

I should cut off your legs.
But for someone with hypo-endocrinal thyro-encephalitis
you sure do have some beautiful walkers.

Since that's not an option!!!

I keep my heart locked away in this rib cage
and I've long since lost the key so...

                              you can't have that.

Since I can't stop you,
I can't outrun you,
I hide behind these walls
but
you stand there.

99

Like,
you're waiting for me to walk out
or for the walls to crumble
like you're some misguided Jericho
shouting at this mammoth edifice of protection
surrounding my dying heart
hoping God will tear them down.

Stop shouting at me!

I'm not coming out there.

Ok,
maybe just for a second
but I don't want to hurt you.

Sometimes when I'm tired of living my life on the run there's a
temptation to succumb to this condition.
No,
I can't give in
my survival is at stake.

Christopher Michael

I WARNED YOU

The sexiest thing about you is your unavailability. The silk rose petals that compose the skin of your legs moves me as much as they move you. I love your long slender fingers, your lips make my imagination melt; I can wash my soul in your eyes, but your unavailability, now that's sexy.

I need you to listen to this, but I hope you're not.

It would behoove you to take note, so please stop reading me.

You're every bit the house the commodores sing about, four walls with bricks of breathtaking beauty, brilliance, benevolence and everything I need, but they're still walls, your love is closing in on me and I can't breathe.

Don't read between the lines, stop filling in the blanks there are none. Just listen to what I'm saying.

I'm a bull in a china shop trying to tip toe past your delicate heart, even though I warned you not to put it on the top shelf right next to me.

I warned you.

It's not about the lies men tell.
It's about the truth women refuse to hear.
I still need time to climb out of the last love I fell in.
Speaking of time.

I can commit to being on time because I'm afraid I may miss something, but I can't commit to you for the same reason.

I warned you.

101

CURRICULUM VITAE
(ABOUT CHRISTOPHER MICHAEL)

1989   Learned how to write poetry

1999   Wrote a poem to impress a girl and discovered he was good at it.
Performed publicly at the Ying Yang in Atlanta Ga.
Introduced to Under One Roof and the Killeen Poetry Scene by Mr. Nice
Entered his first poetry slam and won.

2004   Starts Slamming regularly at Austin Poetry Slam

2005   Wins the Austin City Grand Slam and makes the Austin Slam Team
Kicks off Killeen Poetry Slam with John Crow via The Poet's Ball

2006   Returns as the Austin Slam Champion and a member of the team
Released his first CD titled "The Appetizer"

2007   Killeen Poetry Slam makes its debut coached by Christopher Michael at the
National Poetry Slam missing national champions by 0.4 points bested by Team Charlotte.
Comes in 2nd in the last National Individual Slam after a tie breaker
(Christopher may or may not still be bitter about that one)

2008   Killeen Slam Champion
Killeen Slam Team and Coach

2009   Killeen Slam Team and Coach
Rock The Republic Slam Champion

2010   Coaches Texas Youth Word Collectives Under 21 Slam
Arkansas Grand Slam Champion
Rock The Republic Slam Champion
Releases 2nd CD titled "Poet For Hire"
Killeen Slam Team

2011   After the tragic loss of Sheila Siobhan, Christopher picks up the
leadership mantle of The Austin Youth Slam

Christopher Michael

2012	Returns to Austin Poetry Slam as coach, regular host and member of the board. They Speak Youth Slam Coach
2013	Attempts to take a break from poetry. FAILS!
2014	Austin Slam Team Kicks off his Think, Laugh, Cry Tour Elected to the Executive Council of Poetry Slam Inc.
2015	Finally writes a damn book! Maybe a new CD too. Winner 1st Texas Slam Master Slam
2016	Austin Frontera Fest "Best of Fest" Southern Fried Slam Finalist Austin Mayor Adler declares June 23rd "Christopher Michael Day" Wins The SlamMaster Slam at the 2016 National Poetry Slam Leads Austin NeoSoul to 4th in the nation at NPS Individual World Poetry Slam Haiku Death Match Champion Individual World Poetry Slam Finalist Nominated Texas State Artist (Poet Laureate) but didn't get Failed to produce a new CD (Maybe next year)

Hootie Hooo

310 BROWN STREET .com

Nuclear Orange

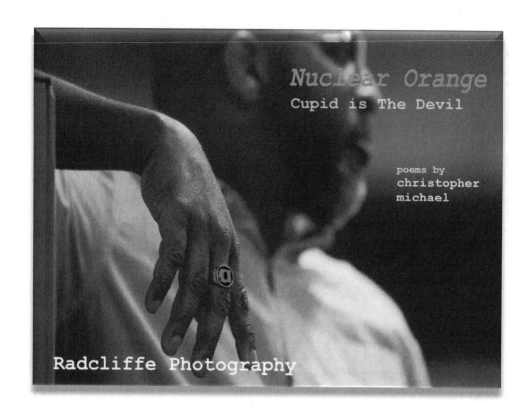

Nuclear Orange
Cupid is The Devil

poems by
christopher
michael

Radcliffe Photography

@mrmichael310

www.mrmichael310.com

Christopher Michael

Made in the USA
San Bernardino, CA
12 January 2017